Machines at Work
Trains

by Rebecca Stromstad Glaser

Bullfrog Books

Ideas for Parents and Teachers

Bullfrog Books give children practice reading informational text at the earliest levels. Repetition, familiar words, and photo labels support early readers.

Before Reading:

- Discuss the cover photo. What does it tell them?

- Look at the picture glossary together. Read and discuss the words.

Read the Book

- "Walk" through the book and look at the photos. Let the child ask questions. Point out the photo labels.

- Read the book to the child, or have him or her read independently.

After Reading

- Prompt the child to think more. Ask: Have you ever watched a freight train? What did it carry? Have you ever ridden a train? What was it like?

Bullfrog Books are published by Jump!
5357 Penn Avenue South
Minneapolis, MN 55419
www.jumplibrary.com

Copyright © 2013 Jump! International copyright reserved in all countries. No part of this book may be reproduced in any form without written permission from the publisher.

Library of Congress Cataloging-in-Publication Data
Glaser, Rebecca Stromstad.
 Trains / by Rebecca Stromstad Glaser.
    pages cm — (Bullfrog books. Machines at work)
 Summary: "This photo-illustrated book for early readers describes the many types of train cars pulled by a freight train and what they are built to carry. Includes picture glossary"—Provided by publisher.
 Includes bibliographical references and index.
 ISBN 978-1-62031-022-9 (hardcover : alk. paper)
 1. Freight cars—Juvenile literature. I. Title.
 TF470.D54 2012
 625.2—dc23   2012009096

Series Designer: Ellen Huber
Photo Researcher: Heather Dreisbach
Book Production: Heather Dreisbach

Photo Credits
Alamy, 15, 23bl; Getty Images, cover, 7;
iStockphoto, 5, 10–11, 12–13, 18–19, 23ml, 23br;
Shutterstock, 1, 3, 4, 6, 8–9, 10, 14, 16–17, 19, 21, 22, 23tl, 23tr, 23mr.

Printed in the United States of America at Corporate Graphics, North Mankato, Minnesota.
7-2012 / PO 1122
10 9 8 7 6 5 4 3 2 1

Table of Contents

Trains at Work

8330 8330

Whoo! Whoo!
A train horn blows.

It is near a crossing.

The gate comes down.

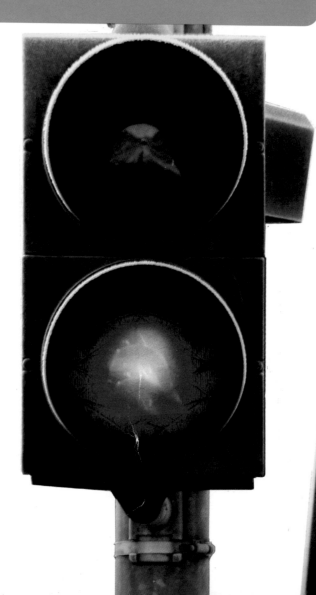

Sam's mom stops the car.
They watch the train.

A train has many cars.

A tank car holds oil.

hatch

A hopper car
holds coal.

Bottom hatches
make it easy
to unload.

THIS CAR EXCESS HEIGHT

2 INCH HF COMP SHOES

LIFT, JACK
AND PULL
HERE

DEFECT CARD

A boxcar is closed.

It keeps things dry.

13

A flatcar is open.

It holds big steel pipes.

14

It can also hold a tractor.

An auto rack
carries cars.

It can hold 10
or more cars.

NACISK KOŁA MAX. 6,0 kN   NOSNOŚĆ PLATFORMY 4500 kg

ROCZNA REWIZJA
URZĄDZENIA DŹWIGOWEGO   918 12.06   Sp   3 REV 918 19.12.06   NACISK KOŁA MAX. 6,0 kN

17

container

A well car holds
containers.

The containers can
be moved to ships.

The train is gone.

The gates go up.

Now we can get home!

WACHT tot het rode licht gedoofd is
er kan nog een trein komen

Parts of a Train

horn
A part that makes a loud, high sound to warn that a train is coming.

locomotive
An engine used to pull train cars.

track
A rail for trains to go on.

Picture Glossary

auto rack
A train car built to hold cars from the factory.

hopper car
A train car that holds coal, sand, rock, or grain.

boxcar
A train car built to keep things dry; it can hold anything that fits inside.

tank car
A round car that holds liquids.

flatcar
A flat train car that holds big, bulky things.

well car
A flat train car with low sides that holds large containers.

Index

To Learn More

Learning more is as easy as 1, 2, 3.

1) Go to www.factsurfer.com

2) Enter "train" into the search box.

3) Click the "Surf" button to see a list of websites.

With factsurfer.com, finding more information is just a click away.